I Wish I Were An

Adventures of an Essenti

Written by
Kiersten Warren
And Ripley

DEDICATION

Dear Children of the world and your pets,

I'm dedicating this to you.
You keep each other's secrets and hold
each other's hands/paws/claws.

Where do shenanigans go when they're not happening?
What becomes of an old snuggle?

They're with your fur, feathered, scaly friends of course.
Right where you left them.

And from there, said shenanigans are tucked into the
sweet thumping chambers of your heart.

To visit with again and again.
Whenever tender needs remembering.

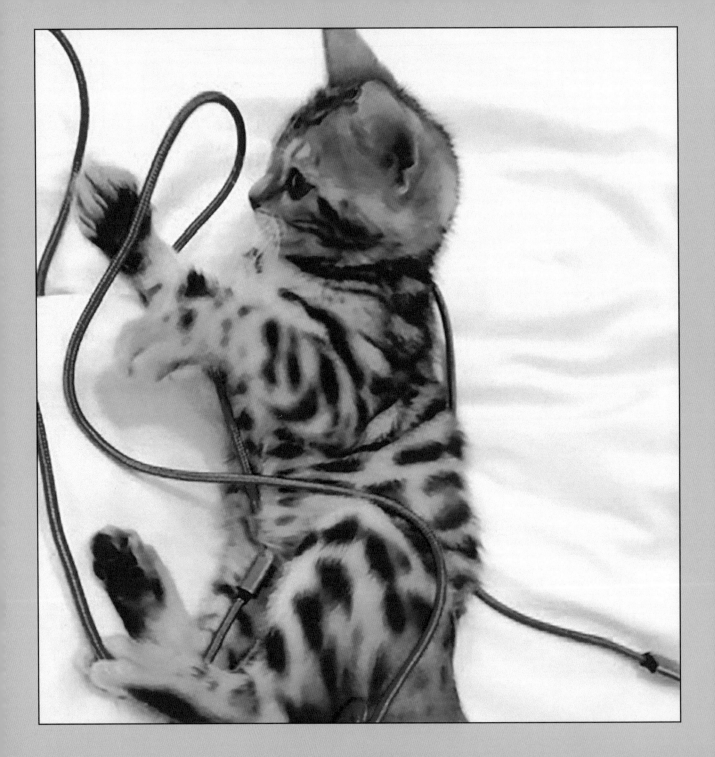

I WISH I WERE
AN OCELOT

I wish I were an ocelot with thunder paws named, Lancelot.

And at your feet
a bird I'd drop.

A feathered result.
What my day wrought.

You'd laugh and squeal,
yet scold me not.

For is only the
nature of Lancelot.

The cleverest hunter,
sheer talent, not taught.

Mummy
scratches
my ears and
counts my
spots.

Do you love me, yes?

Do you love me, not?

Then off I go
in a regal trot.

To find a
fight I've
not yet
fought.

The End.

ABOUT THE AUTHOR
RIPLEY'S PORTION
(Full name is Ripley Karoo Kikaida Comaneci)

Ripley Karoo Kikaida Comaneci is a Bengal kitten with heart shaped markings who came to live with the Warren-Acevedos at the height of Covid lockdown.

The kitten Ripley was aptly named for Sigourney Weaver's character in the movie Alien who taught us that even during times of unspeakable horror one needs to find something small to love.

The rest of kitten's name honors a region in South Africa, a Japanese superhero, and a legendary Romanian gymnast who revolutionized her sport.

ABOUT THE AUTHOR
KIERSTEN'S PORTION

Kiersten Warren is an actress, writer, photographer and dedicated poetic observer.

Ripley has a special treat for you...

Scan the image below and you will see and hear a video of
I Wish I Were An Ocelot being read to you!

Digital Design Services by Telemachus Press, LLC
7652 Sawmill Road, Suite 304
Dublin, Ohio 43016
http://www.telemachuspress.com

ISBN: 978-1-956867-44-2 (eBook)
ISBN: 978-1-956867-45-9 (Paperback)

JUVENILE FICTION / ANIMALS / CATS

Version 2023.02.21

Printed in Great Britain
by Amazon

19316209R00020